Creative Mindfulness:

20+ Strategies for Recovery and Wellness

Prepared by Jamie Marich, Ph.D., LPCC-S, LICDC-CS

Creator of *Dancing Mindfulness*

Founder of *Mindful Ohio*

© 2013

Mindful Ohio

MINDFUL OHIO

Creative Mindfulness:
20+ Strategies for Recovery and Wellness
Mindful Ohio © 2013
Warren, OH
All Rights Reserved

ISBN-13: 978-0615825069
ISBN-10: 0615825060

For more information on *Mindful Ohio* and our programs, please go to
www.mindfulohio.com

Cover & headshot photography by Rebecca Scarpaci
Scarpaci's photographs also featured on exercises 1, 3, 11, 16, 17, 18 & 20

For my clients…

Thank you for being my greatest teachers throughout the years

Table of Contents

Mindfully Yours   1

Core Definitions   4

Practicing Awareness (#1)   7

Belly Breathing (#2)   9

Body Cuing (#3)   11

Light Stream Imagery (#4)   13

Mindful Listening (#5)   15

Energetic Massage (#6)   17

Doodling (#7)   19

Noodling (#8)   21

Mindful Eating (#9)   23

Fully Body Rising (#10)   25

Complete Breathing (#11)   27

Clench and Release (#12)   29

Finding My Marbles (#13)   31

Walking Mindfully (#14)   33

Ocean Breathing (#15)   35

Monkey Tap (#16)   37

The Gaze (#17)   39

"Jam and Bread" to Healthy Posture (#18)   41

Lion Breathing (#19)   43

Dancing Mindfulness (#20)   45

Worksheets to Help You Practice   48

Recommended Reading   53

Acknowledgments   55

About Dr. Jamie   56

Mindfully Yours…

As a woman in recovery from multiple substances and a lifetime of co-dependent responses, the practice of mindfulness helps me heal. Conventional recovery logic encourages us to *stay in today*, and mindfulness practice gives me the strategies for doing just that. As a woman continuing to heal from the imprints of traumatic stress, mindfulness practice is beneficial because it keeps my head from ruminating over past hurts or projecting over future worries. As a professional woman with daily stressors to navigate, the practice of mindfulness is just good common sense…it's a practice that helps me stay grounded amidst the chaos.

Mindfulness derives from the Sanskrit word meaning *awareness*, or in a more nuanced translation, *to come back to awareness*. With its very meaning, mindfulness practice invites us to live in the *now* as a pathway to wellness. The idea seems like good old-fashioned common sense, but modern Western culture is the epitome of mindlessness: fast-paced, externally focused, and outcome-oriented. Mindfulness practice places emphasis on the journey, the *process*, instead of the destination or end result. Through mindful practice, we can cultivate the attitudes of non-striving (i.e., not obsessing over outcome), patience, and trust; attitudes that serve us in our pursuit of wellness.

In his classic book *Wherever You Go, There You Are* (1994), Jon Kabat-Zinn, Ph.D., a leading figure in adopting the ancient Buddhist principles of mindfulness meditation for Western psychology and healthcare defines mindfulness as, *"paying attention in a particular way: on purpose, in the presence of the moment, and non-judgmentally"* (p. 4). My introduction to mindfulness practice acquainted me to this definition. As a recipient and practitioner of a popular psychotherapy for post-traumatic stress called Eye Movement Desensitization and Reprocessing (EMDR), I learned the therapeutic value of noticing without judgment. Francine Shapiro, Ph.D., who created EMDR in 1987, was a student of mindfulness and wove many mindfulness concepts into her EMDR protocol. After years of receiving, practicing, and studying EMDR, it dawned on me that the mindfulness features of the therapy are what I found most helpful. In EMDR, we invite clients to just notice or observe something, such as a thought, a body feeling, a memory, or an emotion; we encourage them to just *notice*, whatever it may be, without judgment. This practice may seem simple, yet where so many approaches to therapy confront irrational beliefs or promote analysis, mindfulness approaches in therapy encourage people to just *notice*. Through this paying attention without fear of judgment or outcome, tremendous healing can result.

My experiences with the mindful features of EMDR prompted me to study mindfulness practice more fully. I learned that although mindfulness practice is Buddhist in its origins because, at its essence, it is the heart of Buddhist meditation, there is nothing specifically Buddhist required to practice it. In other words, you can be totally aware and in the moment with Christian or Jewish practices. You can be in the moment with facets of nature or even with secular elements of living. I recognize there may always be resistance from people devout in their religions who fear mindfulness because of its Buddhist origins. Devout atheists may also object, equating mindfulness solely with spirituality. I encourage you to keep as open of a mind to whatever extent is possible for you. You may be surprised at how healing the practice of simply living in the *now* can be!

Being able to healthfully live in the *now* does not happen instantly. Mindfulness is a practice and it requires just that…practice. Some people need very structured programs, like Kabat-Zinn's classic 8-week Mindfulness-Based Stress Reduction (MBSR). Other people, like me, need to be able to infuse their own sense of creativity and flexibility for the practice to really internalize. I put this book together for people who need trial and error with different channels for attaining mindful awareness. This booklet is not a program or a protocol, it is simply a collection of 20 ideas on how to practice mindfulness and internalize mindful attitudes using a variety of sensory channels. Explore—experiment with the strategies described herein to discover the approach, or series of approaches, that work for you. Find out what you can commit to for regular, daily, real-life practice. For instance, it may not be feasible for you to stop in your tracks at work and meditate for 20-30 minutes. However, you will likely find 2-3 minute consistent pockets to do an exercise like *Clench and Release* (#12). Discover what works for you, but don't be afraid to step out of your comfort zone and in the spirit of non-judgment, try some exercises that you previously dismissed. You may surprise yourself!

You can use this book for your personal practice or to help you work with clients and students more effectively. Each exercise can be photocopied for dissemination with students or clients for learning purposes. My hope is that you will derive both personal and professional benefit from the booklet. Each exercise contains space on the back for journaling or notes about your attempts with the exercise. There are also worksheets at the end of the book where you keep your own inventory on how these exercises best serve you, a bonus feature for those of you who may require more linear structure and guidance.

Core Definitions

mindfulness: paying attention in a particular way: on purpose, in the presence of the moment, and non-judgmentally (Kabat-Zinn, 1994/2005) ; comes from the Sanskrit word meaning "awareness," specifically, "coming back to awareness"

Seven Primary Attitudes of Mindfulness

non-judging: thinking, feeling, or responding absent the influence of an internal sensor or critic; an attitude of "just noticing" thoughts, emotions, or whatever may surface as relevant. Non-judgment, however, does not endorse behaviors that put yourself or others in harm's way.

patience: derives from the Latin root meaning to *undergo, suffer, or bear*; the art of deferring gratification; waiting.

beginner's mind: *beginner* comes from the same Middle English root as *to open*; beginner's mind is approaching each new task with an open mind. Think of the sense of wonder that a child attempting a task for the first time may experience; removing the expert's mindset, refraining from acting on a proverbial auto pilot mode.

trust: having belief in some unseen entity, an outcome, another person or group, or the internal self

non-striving: thinking, feeling, or acting with focus on the process, not just the outcome. Non-striving does not imply laziness or sloth; think of it as an attitude that encourages you, even in your work, to not force, to refrain from trying so hard. Letting whatever happens, happen

acceptance: a coming to terms with reality, no matter how harsh or unpleasant it may be; doing so can be a pathway to peace. Does not imply you have to "like" the reality that you discontinue fighting.

letting go: releasing your "grip" on a situation, emotion, person, thing, or outcome, generally resulting in a freeing response (or at least the beginnings of one)

Other Attitudes of Mindfulness (Flowing From Cultivation of the Primaries)

friendliness	gratitude
gentleness	curiosity
non-attachment	non-reactivity
happiness	creativity
attunement	persistence
confidence	willingness

Photograph by Rebecca Scarpaci

Notes:

1.) Practicing Awareness

Too often in life we beat ourselves up with messages like, "I just can't pay attention." Rest assured, you are not alone…it takes practice. This exercise is a basic gateway for learning mindfulness and to begin *practicing* it.

- Shift around in your chair a little bit, or in a seated position on the ground, until you find a position that, for you, symbolizes paying attention.

- Be careful not to slouch your shoulders, but also be aware not to sit so straight up that it hurts you to be in this sitting posture.

- Spend some time paying attention to your body and make a mental note of what this posture of awareness feels like for you.

- If your head starts to wander or you feel that you've stopped paying attention, **that's okay!** It's a chance to practice **non-judgment** and **beginner's mind**. When you catch yourself, just use this as a chance to bring your attention back to that body posture of awareness.

- Work up to practicing this in three-minute increments. This practice is a wonderful way to cultivate the attitude of **patience.**

Taking the modifications and creativity further…

- ✓ If three minutes is attempted and simply can't be done, consider adding in another sensory element and practice paying attention to that element (e.g., a scent, like an oil, spice, or candle; a simple sound, like something from a nature sounds CD; a tactile sensation, like holding a rock, a marble, or a stuffed animal).

- ✓ If sitting doesn't work, this same exercise can also be done standing up or lying down. Remember to keep the emphasis on that word 'awareness'…you can lay down with awareness!

Journal/Notes on This Exercise:

2.) Belly Breathing

Have you ever watched an infant breathe? If so, you will notice that babies naturally breathe with their bellies…somewhere along the way we seem to lose this natural tendency and develop rapid, shallow breathing that originates in the chest. Like with all elements of mindfulness, belly breathing takes practice!

- Put one or both hands on the upper area of your stomach so that you can really pay attention to the motions you are engaging with your diaphragm
- As you inhale with your nose, allow your belly to expand as far as it will go
- Exhale with your mouth, allowing the belly to pull back in
- Continue this inhale-exhale pattern and your own pace, giving it at least 6-7 sets to find a rhythm and style that works for you…**curiosity** and **non-judgment** are key…find what works for you!
- After finding your rhythm, consider puckering your mouth and really exaggerating your exhale, striving to make it somewhat longer than your inhale…this ought to help you relax even more.

Taking the modifications and creativity further…

- ✓ If you feel awkward or in any way out of control with this suggested pattern, consider starting with an exhale instead of the inhale.
- ✓ If paying attention to the breath on its own is not working for you, consider adding a count to it (e.g., In-2-3-4…hold…Out 2-3-4). You can also add a word or a special phrase (e.g., "Satnam;" "Amen," "Help me")...the possibilities are endless.
- ✓ You can really engage children in this practice by having them put something like a Beanie Baby or a flatter type of stuffed animal on their stomach so they have a focus point while they observe the rise and fall of the belly.

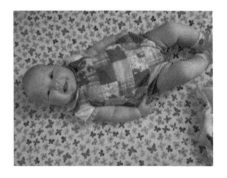

Journal/Notes on This Exercise:

3.) Body Cuing

Learning to pay attention to the messages that your body gives you is a vital part of wellness. Body cuing is a modification of the mindfulness practice of *body scan*. It helps you to pay better attention to your body and listen to what it needs in any given moment. We are covering this skill early because it is used in combination with other skills we're going to cover today.

- Bring to mind something that stresses you out. It doesn't have to be a major trauma, but something that you identify as stressful.

- Spend a few moments reflecting on that stressor. What does it look like? Does it have a sound or any other sensory qualities?

- Now, notice what is happening in your body…does the stress seem to be felt in one part of your body, or maybe in one organ specifically? Or is the stressor all over your body?

- There are no *right* or *wrong* answers, just practice **acceptance** of what is going on in your body right now. Spend a few moments just sitting with the stressor, just noticing the body response, in a spirit of **non-judgment**.

- If you want, begin describing the presence of that stressor in your body: If it had a color, what color would it be? If it had a shape, what shape would it be? If it had a texture, what would that texture be? Are there any other qualities, like temperature, sound, or smell?

- Now ask yourself, what does my body need the most right now to help the presence of this body stress? Even if your gut-level answer doesn't seem to be the healthiest response, practice **non-judgment**, just notice what your body needs.

Taking the modifications and creativity further…

- ✓ Consider drawing the experience of stress in your body; young people may find this approach more appealing or accessible then having to describe it. Colored pencils, crayons, markers, or other crafting elements can be employed.

Journal/Notes on This Exercise:

4.) Light Stream Imagery

Using the visual power of your imagination can be remarkably healing, especially to clear out some of the body-level distress that you've identified and have learned to pay attention to. Here is a very simple *guided imagery* exercise that you can use:

- Imagine that a bright and healing light has begun to form overhead. This light can be whatever color you want it to be, whatever you associate with healing, **happiness,** goodness, or any of the other attitudes of mindfulness. If you don't like the idea of a light, you can think of it simply as a color or an essence.

- Now, think about this light beginning to move through your body or over your body (your choice), from the top of your head, moving inch-by-inch, slowly, until it reaches the bottom of your feet.

- If you want, you can think about this light grounding you safely into the earth.

- Spend a few moments just hanging out with the presence of this light or essence in your body. Notice if it has any other qualities besides color, like a texture or a sound or a smell.

- Draw your attention back to where you first cued your body stress…what's happened to it?

- If the distress is still there on some level in your body, think about deepening your belly breathing so it makes the light or essence more brilliant and intense…so brilliant and intense that the distress can't even dream of existing within it.

- Keep practicing the exercise, in the attitude of **patience** if you don't notice much of a shift the first time.

Taking the modifications and creativity further…

- ✓ If you have a spiritual belief system, you can imagine that light coming from a spiritual source (e.g., heaven, God/Jesus, the universe, etc.)
- ✓ The light/essence can enter anywhere in the body. For instance, if your chest anxiety is very high, it may feel more appropriate to have the light enter there.
- ✓ If the light stream image by itself is hard to keep in focus, add another sensory element to enhance the focus (e.g., smell, simple sound or music, tactile sensation).

Journal/Notes on This Exercise:

5.) Mindful Listening

Sound is such vital part of our world, but when is the last time you have really taken a chance to pay attention to what you are hearing? Mindful listening is a wonderful way to practice mindfulness; it can be very stress relieving once you engage in some **curiosity** to find the right sound or sounds that work for you, and mindful listening can also help you clear out any body level distress that's manifesting.

- Start with finding a simple nature sound, or series of sounds…you can do this by finding a sample on a recording, or going to a place in nature where you know a sample will exist (e.g., the park).

- Begin practicing single-pointed concentration on that sound…for the next three minutes or so, your only job is to listen to that sound. Once again, if your attention wanders be **patient** and **gentle** with yourself…just use those moments as an opportunity to draw your attention back to the sound.

- Notice what happens! If your first sound choice didn't pan out, **persist** and keep experimenting…there are thousands of sounds and sound combinations you can try until you find what works for you.

Taking the modifications and creativity further…

- ✓ Actual pieces of music may work better then nature sounds. For some people, simple, hypnotic/meditative music may do the trick, for others, more dynamic sounds may be what engage them fully. Others still may really benefit from music with lyrics. Trial and error until you find what works for you…find what helps you to really be drawn in to your listening experience so hopefully any manifestations of stress will clear.

- ✓ For hearing impaired clients, the benefits of this exercise can still be achieved by sitting close to large speakers and letting the vibrations do the work.

Journal/Notes on This Exercise:

6.) Energetic Massage

Do you ever feel, quite literally like your brain hurts? Wouldn't it be great if you could give your brain a massage? With a simple mindfulness exercise that harnesses the power of your own tactile energy, you can!

- Rub your hands together for at least thirty seconds (you can go longer if you want). Really work up some heat!
- Pull your hands apart and bring them to your forehead…there are many variations. You can close your eyes, and place the base of your palms over your eyes; let the rest of your hands curl over your forehead to the top of the forehead. Or you can rest the base of your palms on your cheeks and go around your eyes.
- Settle in, feel the energy you generated in your hands move into your brain. Just **let go** and let the energy work in you….practice **non-striving**.
- Hold as long as you like.

Taking the modifications and creativity further…

- ✓ You can bring the energy from your hands to any part of your body that is feeling tense or anxious. Think about bringing the heat energy from your hands to your chest or stomach if you are noticing any tension or pain.
- ✓ The 'cranial hold' position is an option after generating the energy. To achieve this, horizontally bring one hand to your forehead and the other hand to the back of your head.
- ✓ Consider adding another sense into the process for optimal relaxation, like meditative music, or an aromatherapy oil of your choice.

Journal/Notes on This Exercise:

7.) Doodling

Mindless doodling is a popular way to pass the time when we are bored in class or in a seminar. But have you ever thought of using mindful doodling as a way to cope with stress and explore your **creativity**?

- Get a blank piece of paper and a writing utensil.
- Begin by drawing a standard shape of your choice, like a circle or a square...but don't just draw it to get it done...really take your time and be mindful of the movement in your hand and the image you see appearing on the paper.
- Once you close the shape, just start moving your hand...think about letting your breath connect with your drawing hand and just notice what happens. Practice **beginner's mind** and **non-striving**.
- Take at least three minutes, and just go...be mindful of what you are drawing. Really stay connected to it visually and get lost in your art as your mind allows.
- After three minutes, put the writing utensil down but stay visually connected to your piece for a few moments longer. Just notice what you notice, and pay attention to what happens in your body and head.

Taking the modifications and creativity further...

- ✓ Be crafty! Consider using multiple colors, writing utensils, paint, or textured implements (e.g., remember puffy paint?)
- ✓ Put music on as you do this and see what happens with your doodling and your experience if you let your breath *and* the music connect with your creating hand.

Journal/Notes on This Exercise:

8.) Noodling

Haven't you ever envied a cooked noodle? The way it just slithers free and easy, without stress is an admirable quality that can teach us how to practice the attitude of **letting go**. Think of how fun, and potentially beneficial, it could be, to take on the roll of a noodle.

- For optimal benefit, come to your feet (although you can also do this sitting or lying down).
- With your next breath, think of taking on the role of a noodle…it's suggested that you begin in your shoulders and then let the 'noodling' move through the rest of your body.
- Keep *noodling*, in a mindful way, practicing **beginner's mind, non-judgment,** and **non-striving** for at least three minutes.
- When you've completed, allow yourself to be still for a few moments longer (standing, sitting, or lying down)…notice how it feels!

Taking the modifications and creativity further…

- ✓ Although you can do this in silence, it is lots of fun if you put on some music that can bring out your inner noodle!
- ✓ This exercise can be fun with props like scarves or ribbons.

Thanks to Cornelius Hubbard, Jr. for his help in designing this exercise.

Journal/Notes on This Exercise:

9.) Mindful Eating

In our culture, we seem to eat on autopilot…it's no wonder that there's an epidemic of obesity and other gastrointestinal problems. Mindful eating is the answer to so many of these problems. The art of mindful eating encompasses: a.) slowing down, b.) really paying attention, c.) being **attuned** to each sense in order to fully savor the experience. Popular food items for completing this exercise include almonds, raisins, and dark chocolate. However, using an item that needs to be unwrapped can add another dimension to the sensory experience.

- Hold the item in your hand. Look at it, really observe it. Notice every little detail of what you see.
- Roll the item around in your hands and notice what the wrapper feels like and what it sounds like.
- As slowly as you are physically able, begin to unwrap the packaging, paying attention to every sense along the way, especially the sound. Place the wrapper aside.
- Look at the edible item in your hand, noticing what it looks like, rolling it around in your hand, bringing it up to your nose to smell it.
- Very slowly, bring the item to your mouth and rub it over your lips, noticing whatever you notice, then putting it in your mouth. Just allow the item to sit on your tongue for a few minutes. Be **curious**. Bring the item to the roof of your mouth, roll it around the sides of your mouth.
- Before biting into or swallowing the object, be sure to take some swallows and notice any juiciness or other tastes coming from the item.
- Mindfully take your first bite into the item, noticing what it sounds like, what it feels like, what it tastes like…maybe you even notice a surge in the smell.
- Continue at this slow pace, savoring each sensation, down to the last gulp or swallow.

Taking the modifications and creativity further…

✓ Do this with a whole meal…notice if you feel fuller, sooner.

Journal/Notes on This Exercise:

Journal/Notes on This Exercise:

10.) Full Body Rising

Standing up, for those of us with full leg function, is an action we do so mindlessly we take it for granted. However, it can feel really, really good if we pay attention to rising slowly, and with purpose. Whenever we do an activity that is normally so automatic in a slow, mindful way, it is a perfect chance to cultivate the attitude of **patience**.

- While in a sitting position, allow your upper body to fold over your seated, lower body. Your feet don't have to touch the ground, but aim there. Take a few moments and notice how it feels when the blood moves to your head as you fold over.
- Very slowly and carefully, allow your buttocks to lift off of the chair while remaining in the bent over position. If your hands can touch your feet or the ground, do that; if not, just allow your hands to fall wherever they may on your legs.
- Hang out in this folded over, "rag doll" position as long as you are able.
- Slowly, mindfully begin to unfold your spine and rise…think one vertebra at a time…avoid just rushing up.
- When you have totally unfolded, let your shoulder roll back and gaze straight ahead, with confidence. Notice how you feel.
- Take this confidence into the world!

Taking the modifications and creativity further…

- ✓ If you are unable to stand, you can still achieve the benefits of this exercise by doing the first part of bending over and then unfolding the spine…take the confidence stance with your upper body, even in a seated position.
- ✓ Putting on some music that creates a vibe of rising or emergence (e.g., think tunes from "The Lion King" or similar themes) to really enhance the mood of growing in to confidence.

Journal/Notes on This Exercise:

11.) Complete Breathing

Think of a complete breath as a three-part breath, with the diaphragmatic part of the breath being the first step. In essence, complete breath, as the name suggests, is a fuller breath.

- Begin with a diaphragmatic breath but continue the inhale into the ribs and then the chest. You can put a hand on the chest to help with your awareness.
- At the top of the inhale, cradle the breath in your awareness for a moment; this is a more meditative way to conceptualize holding your breath.
- Gradually release the breath with your exhale, allowing the chest, the ribs, and the belly to pull back in.
- Continue this inhale-exhale pattern at your own pace, giving it at least 6-7 sets to find a rhythm and style that works for you…**curiosity** and **non-judgment** are key, like with any other breath.

Taking the modifications and creativity further…

- ✓ The standard pattern with exhales is to keep them slow and deliberate. However, a very powerful variation is to do a fast, dramatic exhale, like a "sigh of relief."
- ✓ Feel free to get as a dramatic as you want on the exhale, perhaps bringing the hand to the forehead…really think of this breath as a chance to put **letting go** of negative energy into practice.
- ✓ When you expand your chest on the inhale, you can bring up "superhero" imagery (especially fun to do with kids) to further the empowering motion.

Journal/Notes on This Exercise:

12.) Clench and Release

Have you ever been so angry or stressed you just want to make fists and hit something? In this exercise, you'll be able to do that first…and then practice mindfully **letting go**!

- Make fists.
- As you focus on your clenched fists, bring to mind something that stresses you out.
- As you reflect on the stressor, really notice the contraction of your muscles. Feel your fingernails dig into your skin if possible.
- Whenever it feels too uncomfortable for you to keep holding on, know that you can slowly, mindfully **let go** at any time.
- Notice your fingers uncurling, and feel the trickle of letting go all through your arms, up to your shoulders.
- Notice how good it feels to **let go**!

Taking the modifications and creativity further…

- ✓ Any muscle group can be clenched and released, especially if clenching the fists is too painful or not possible due to context or physical limitations. Clenching and releasing the stomach and feet are other popular choices.
- ✓ For help with sleep and deeper relaxation, clench and release one muscle group at a time (holding each clench 20-30 seconds and then slowly releasing). The entire exercise should take about 20 minutes.
- ✓ Add a relaxing sound (e.g., nature sound, music) in the background, or use an aromatherapy diffuser if you are using this exercise for sleep.

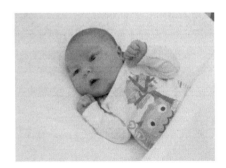

29

Journal/Notes on This Exercise:

13.) Finding My Marbles

We often call going crazy "losing our marbles." However, once we literally find a marble, we can discover that it's a wonderful item to help us cultivate mindful practice through all of our senses.

- Imagine that this is the first time you are ever looking at this type of object…approach it with the spirit of **beginner's mind.** Take the marble in your hand and observe the color. Practice **patience** and spend several minutes just noticing what you notice about the colors and patterns.
- Notice the weight of the marble in your hand. Try moving from hand to hand and notice if there are any differences.
- Roll the marble around in your hands. Observe the texture of the marble against your skin.
- Notice if you hear any sounds.
- Repeat as many times as necessary, practicing **curiosity** with each set.

Taking the modifications and creativity further…

- ✓ Any object can be used for this exercise, especially objects that are meaningful to a client. The key is to think of an object that we ordinarily take for granted, yet upon examination, contains new wonder.
- ✓ Popular options include 12-step recovery coins, chips, or tags, thimbles, and other small toys that might have special significance to a child.

Journal/Notes on This Exercise:

14.) Walking Meditation

For those of us who are physically able, walking is something we take for granted. Yet breaking down something we normally experience as automatic can be incredibly meditative.

- Think about looking towards the horizon during the walk instead of down at your feet.
- Consider the art of breaking this walk down into slow motion, as if you are experiencing it for the first time (**beginner's mind**).
- Standing tall, let your heel connect with the earth and allow the front part of your foot to point towards the sky.
- Very slowly step down, shifting the weight from your heel to the ball of the foot.
- Shift the weight from the ball to the toes.
- Deliberately repeat this same motion on the other foot.
- Continue taking this walk in this slow, deliberate fashion, observing each sensation with a new awareness. Let your walk truly be an exercise in mindful meditation.

Taking the modifications and creativity further...

- ✓ This exercise can be done inside or outside (it is gorgeous to do it outside...nature *is* therapy!)
- ✓ It is recommended that you teach this exercise to a client at a slow pace first, however, the same exercise can be done in the spirit of silence and meditation at a faster pace. This faster pace is good when teaching the idea that we can still achieve mindful awareness even at the *regular* pace of life.

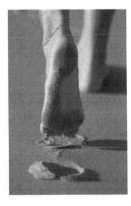

Journal/Notes on This Exercise:

15.) Ocean Breathing (aka, 'Darth Vader' Breathing)

We learn many therapeutically beneficial breaths as inhaling through the nose, exhaling through the mouth. Ocean breath is fundamentally different because it is in through the nose, out through the nose. If you make a certain formation with your mouth and throat, you can **create** the sound of the ocean, right within yourself! Or, you may like to think of this sound as the infamous character, Darth Vader. This breath is excellent for endurance of stress, physical or mental.

- Pucker your mouth like you're sucking through a straw or about to kiss someone. Attempt to contract the back of your throat slightly closed.
- Inhale with your nose; your belly ought to expand with this motion.
- Exhale with your nose; although air will flow out of your mouth, think about doing the work with your nose.
- If your mouth is puckered and throat is contracted, you ought to be hearing the sound of the ocean within you
- Attempt to keep the inhales and exhales even, especially while you're first learning the breath.
- Do not attempt more than five full sets during your first attempt if you are new to this breath.
- It is completely normal if you feel somewhat light headed, but it should be a "good" light-headed. If it does not feel good, chances are you tried too many too soon, or the inhales and exhales were uneven.

Taking the modifications and creativity further...

- ✓ You can envision many different characters with this breath, like Darth Vader, or a charging bull "huffing and puffing" ...**let go** and clear out the negative!
- ✓ Get a mirror and see the steam of your breath or your surface (young people like this especially), **attuning** you to this idea of your breath as "the Force"
- ✓ You can visualize, on any breath, that you are breathing in a calming or soothing color and breathing out a color that represents stress

Journal/Notes on This Exercise:

16.) Monkey Tap (aka, Butterfly Hug)

In nature, primates cross their arms over their chest and tap their shoulders in an alternating nature to self-soothe. In this exercise, we will duplicate this exercise in a mindful way as a way of being **gentle** with ourselves and practice self-soothing.

- Cross your arms over your chest.
- Begin tapping your hands against your body in a slow, deliberate, alternating fashion…think of the same slow pace as the walking meditation since tapping quickly can actually induce anxiety.
- Tap for about a minute and then return your hands to your lap or the table and just breathe for a few moments. Repeat as many sets as needed for relaxation.

Taking the modifications and creativity further…

- ✓ Also this exercise can be mindful and calming in and of itself by simply, mindfully focusing on the tapping, pairing the tapping with a calming scent, a pleasant thought, a positive cognition, or any other positive experience can be sensory paradise!
- ✓ Laurel Parnell's book *Tapping In* is an excellent resource to check out for a variety of ideas on how imageries and other positive material can be "installed" into the brain using this bilateral tapping motion.

Journal/Notes on This Exercise:

17.) The Gaze

In yoga, your gaze is called your *drishti*, and holding this gaze for an extended period of time while in a pose is known to quiet the mind.

- Find a place to gaze, at least one foot in front of you on the floor, or on the wall. If you're lying on your back, you can find a place on the ceiling.
- As you breathe, literally have a staring contest with your chosen spot. Even if you have the desire to look away, see this as an opportunity to practice **patience** and **persistence**.
- After you break your gaze, close your eyes for a moment to reset. Notice if there are any shifts or heightened experiences of relaxation.

Taking the modifications and creativity further…

- ✓ Toys or objects can be a very fun way to practice this focusing exercise. With young children, you can invite them to literally engage in a staring contest with a stuffed animal…it's fun!
- ✓ If you or those you work with have a strong tendency to dissociate (zone out), shorten the periods that you spend in the gaze, or ensure that there is some music on to help you stay healthfully grounded.
- ✓ To find the ideal spot for you, slowly track your eyes from the left side of the wall (or ceiling) in an alternating fashion. When your eyes detect the one position on the wall or ceiling that induces optimal relaxation, use that as your gaze.
- ✓ An emerging approach in the treatment of trauma is called brainspotting, developed by David Grand, as an off-shoot of EMDR. If you like this strategy, you may want to check out his work.

Journal/Notes on This Exercise:

18.) "Jam and Bread" to Healthy Posture

There are tens of thousands of nerve endings in your hands. In yoga, this logic is used for healing through *mudra*, or a hand posture that is made for a meditative purpose. Popular ones include *angeli mudra*, or the famous "prayer" position. Try this one: it looks like the famous "tea I drink with jam and bread" posture from the movie *The Sound of Music*.

- Really notice the tension created in your shoulders as you attempt to pull the hands apart. Notice the friction in your fingers.
- Allow the slight tension in your shoulders to lift and bring your posture into a position of heightened **awareness** and **confidence**.
- When you feel ready, release the hold of your hands, but keep the shoulders in that same position.

Taking the modifications and creativity further…

- ✓ This is an excellent exercise if you struggle with healthy assertiveness and confidence. When you are feeling down about your confidence, practice this mudra to quite literally put your posture into a more assertive place. Hence, it's a great exercise to do before you walk into a tricky situation.
- ✓ Amy Weintraub's *Yoga Skills for Therapists* is an excellent resource for learning more of these neat mudra exercises.

Journal/Notes on This Exercise:

19.) Lion Breathing

Although taking on the full character of a lion is optional with this exercise, allowing yourself to make the face of a lion with this breath can help you with **letting go** of negative energy.

- Begin with a healthy inhale (what you learned in complete breathing).

- Exhale vigorously, allowing the tongue to hang out. Feel the jaw and cheeks loosen. Open the eyes widely to help with this **letting go**.

- Try at least 5 sets, although you can continue with this breath as long as is physically comfortable for you.

Taking the modifications and creativity further...

- ✓ This is a wonderful exercise to teach to children (or adults who aren't too self-conscious to try it). You can think of making this face when ugly thoughts about trauma or stress come up...think about embodying the strength of a lion in the wake of a painful trigger!

Journal/Notes on This Exercise:

20.) *Dancing Mindfulness*

Dancing Mindfulness uses the art of dance as the primary medium of discovering mindful awareness. Dancing through seven primary areas of mindfulness in motion: breath, sound, body, story, mind, spirit, and integrated experience, with a respect to the **attitudes of mindfulness**, participants tap into their body's own healing resources and realize that we all have a unique creativity just waiting to be cultivated!

Although developed as a formal practice by Dr. Marich, it is not a brand name, it is a concept, a way to practice mindful awareness. Literally, you can engage in personal practice in the following way:

- Spend some time with a mindful breath of your choice, working your way into some body cuing.

- Introduce some music into your experience; you can do this by turning on a radio, starting your iPod, or making a playlist in advance along a theme and then beginning that playlist.

- Begin moving organically in a way that connects your breath, to the music, to the body….in essence, if you've ever cranked up music and danced around the house just to get the stress out (**letting go**), you have practiced *Dancing Mindfulness*. The key is to move with intention and focus on staying in the moment with your movements.

- For your practice to truly be *Dancing Mindfulness*, regardless of how long it is, make sure to spend some time in body stillness at the end (in yoga, this is called *sivasana*), letting your breath, the music, and your body integrate the fruits of your practice.

Taking the modifications and creativity further…

- ✓ *Dancing Mindfulness* group classes are fun. Even without formal training, you can practice *Dancing Mindfulness* as an activity with friends or as an activity within a therapeutic setting, as long as people keep a commitment to safe physical and emotional practice. Having a leader to keep the group experience organized and on task with mindful focus is recommended.

Journal/Notes on This Exercise:

Some shots from *Dancing Mindfulness*. Go to www.DancingMindfulness.com for video and for more information about formal training in the practice.

Notes:

Worksheets to Help You Practice

Make Copies if you need; although you may not like or benefit from all of these worksheets, see if using any of them will help you to stay more organized and focused as you begin practicing Creative Mindfulness ☺

Stressors I am Likely to Experience   Strategies That Help the Most

My Favorite Strategies   Time of Day for Practice/Situations to Use

The 5 Senses	Strategies That Help Me Connect

Sight/Visual

Sound/Hearing

Touch/Tactile

Smell/Olfactory

Taste/Gustatory

Combinations?

Recommended Reading

On Mindfulness

Kabat-Zinn, J. (1990). *Full-catastrophe living: Using the wisdom of the body and mind to face stress, pain, and illness.* New York: Delta/Random House.

Kabat-Zinn, J. (2005). *Wherever you go, there you are.* (10th anniversary edition). New York: Hyperion.

Kabat-Zinn, J. (2006). *Coming to our senses: Healing ourselves and the world through mindfulness.* New York: Hyperion.

Kabat-Zinn, J. (2011). *Mindfulness for beginners: Reclaiming the present moment-and your life.* Boulder, CO: Sounds True Books.

Ryan, T. (2012). *A mindful nation: How a simple practice can help us reduce stress, improve performance, and recapture the American spirit.* Carlsbad, CA: Hay House.

On Therapeutic Value of Yoga, Movement, & Spirituality

Emerson, D. & Hopper, E. (2011). *Overcoming trauma with yoga: Reclaiming Your Body.* Berekely, CA: North Atlantic Books.

Hawk, K. (2012). *Yoga and the 12-step path.* Las Vegas, NV: Central Recovery Press.

Weintraub, A. (2004). *Yoga for depression.* New York: Broadway Books.

Weintraub, A. (2012). *Yoga skills for therapists: Effective practices for mood management.* New York: W.W. Norton.

On Trauma and Innovative Methods for Treating/Understanding It

Burana, L. (2009). *I love a man in uniform: A memoir of love, war, and other battles.* New York: Weinstein Books.

Grey, E. (2010). *Unify your mind: Connecting the feelers, thinkers, & doers of your brain.* Pittsburgh, PA: CMH&W, Inc.

Naparstek, B. R. (2004). *Invisible heroes: Survivors of trauma and how they heal.* New York: Bantam Books.

Marich, J. (2012). *Trauma and the twelve steps: A complete guide for enhancing recovery.* Warren, OH: Cornersburg Media.

Parnell, L. (2008). *Tapping in: A step-by-step guide to healing your inner resources through bilateral stimulation.* Boulder, CO: Sounds True Books.

Pease Banitt, S. (2012). The trauma toolkit: Healing PTSD from the inside out. Wheaton, IL: Quest Books.

For complete literature reviews of mindfulness research and practice, visit:

Center for Investigating Healthy Minds
www.investigatinghealthyminds.org/cihmFindings.html

The Greater Good Science Center at UC Berkeley
www.greatergood.berkeley.edu

Mindfulness Research Guide
www.mindfulexperience.org

Mindfulness Research Monthly
http://www.mindfulexperience.org/newsletter.php

Acknowledgments

I could not do what I do without the support, encouragement, and collaboration from the village of people in my life. You all contribute to the work I do in a unique and special way. A few of you deserve special mention when it comes to this project:

- Dr. Kimberly Beck, who quite literally commissioned this book when she asked me to deliver a training on this topic. This booklet, quite literally, exists because of you, and I thank you from the bottom of my heart!

- David Reiter, my husband, my "sun and stars" who lights my life with encouragement and love...we walk this path together!

- My assistant, Allison Bugzavich...there are no words.

- Trish Taylor and Kathy Barecca, friends and protégés, for your unwavering support of this work.

- Maureen Lauer-Gatta, my friend and collaborator, the "yin" to my "yang"...again, there are no words.

- All of my *Dancing Mindfulness* facilitators for your faith in this work, your adventurous spirits, and for teaching me more than I ever could have taught myself about the practice.

- Linda Jackson and Claire Zelasko of CMI Education; talking to the two of you is always a brainstorm of possibilities. I thank you for your continued faith in me.

- Cornelius Hubbard, my one-time student and present-day friend and collaborator...thanks for teaching me how to noodle!

- Annabelle "Belly" Bugzavich, my goddaughter and baby model for this book...she teaches me about mindfulness every time I see her!

- Joy and Misty, my feline daughters...also my teachers of yoga and mindfulness.

About Dr. Jamie Marich

Be sure to visit all of our websites:

www.mindfulohio.com (Also on Facebook)

www.dancingmindfulness.com (Also on Facebook)

www.TraumaTwelve.com (Also on Facebook)

www.jamiemarich.com

www.drjamiemarich.com

Also From Cornersburg Media/Mindful Ohio

Books:

Trauma and the Twelve Steps: A Complete Guide to Enhancing Recovery

by Dr. Jamie Marich (2012)

Music by Jamie Marich:

Grace of a Woman (2012)

Under My Roof (2004)

Give Us Your Peace (2002)

5572031R00037

Made in the USA
San Bernardino, CA
12 November 2013